all woman

VOLUME THREE

International MUSIC Publications

Series Editor: Anna Joyce

Editorial, production and recording: Artemis Music Limited
Design and Production: Space DPS Limited

Published 2001

International Music Publications Limited
Griffin House 161 Hammersmith Road London W6 8BS England

2

Almaz

Words and Music by
Randy Crawford

haunt her,   Al - maz,   you luck-y,   luck-y   thing.___

2. Now   I   watch
3. He throws her

___   Al - maz,___   you___ luck-y,   luck-y   thing.___

3. He throws her kisses, she shares his wishes,
   I'm sure he's keen without a doubt.
   With love so captive, so sorely captive,
   I ask if I could play the part.

Big Spender

Words by Dorothy Fields
Music by Cy Coleman

8

Backing

Crazy For You

Words & Music by
John Bettis and Jon Lind

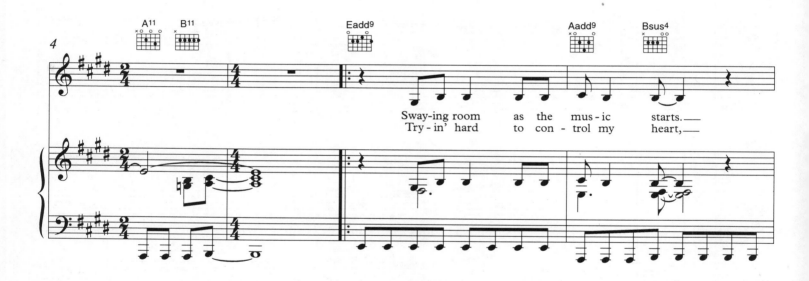

Sway-ing room   as the mus-ic   starts.____
Try-in' hard   to con-trol my   heart,____

Stran-gers mak-ing the most____ of the dark.____   Two by two their   bod-
I walk ov-er to where____ you____ are.____   Eye to eye, we   need

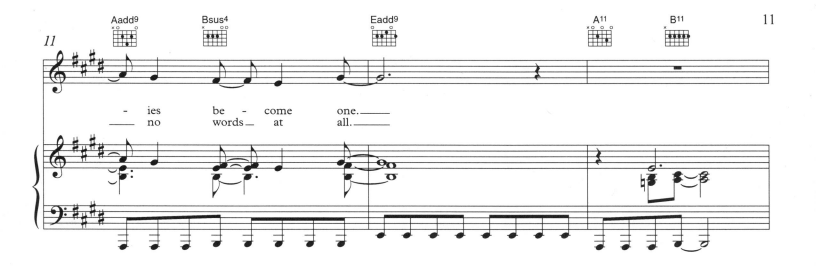

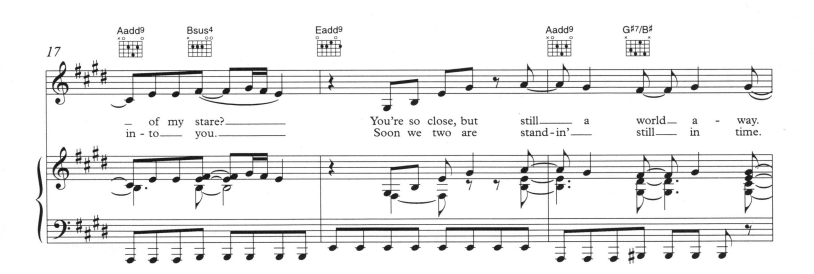

14

Fame

Words by Dean Pitchford
Music by Michael Gore

From A Distance

Backing

Words and Music by Julie Gold

3. From a distance, you look like my friend
   Even though we are at war.
   From a distance I just cannot comprehend
   What all this fighting is for.
   From a distance there is harmony
   And it echoes through the land.
   It's the hope of hopes, it's the love of loves.
   It's the heart of every man.

Nina Simone

Backing

My Baby Just Cares For Me

Words by Gus Kahn
Music by Walter Donaldson

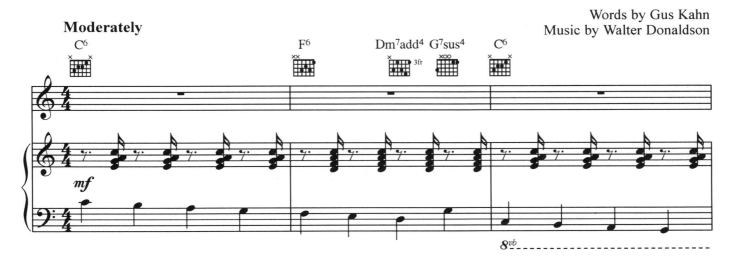

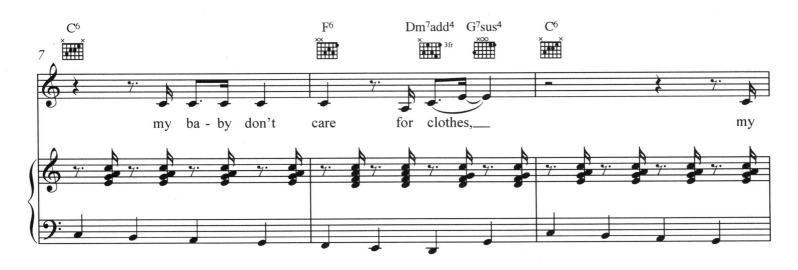

My Funny Valentine

Words by Lorenz Hart
Music by Richard Rodgers

33

34

Promise Me

Words and Music by
Beverley Craven

The Power Of Love

Words and Music by
Candy De Rouge, Gunther Mende,
Jennifer Rush and Mary Susan Applegate

Backing

Respect

Solid 4 beat

Words and Music by Otis Redding

What you want ba - by I got.
I ain't gon - na do you wrong while you gone.

What you want you know I got it.
I ain't gon - na do you wrong 'cause I don't wan - na.

Take My Breath Away

Words and Music by
Giorgio Moroder and Tom Whitlock

1. Watch - ing ev - ery mo - tion in____ my fool - ish lov - er's game;____
2. Watch - ing, I keep wait - ing, still____ an - ti - ci - pat - ing love,____
3. *see block lyrics*

on this end - less o - cean, fi -
nev - er he - si - tat - ing to____

3. Watching every motion in this foolish lover's game;
   Haunted by the notion somewhere there's a love in flames.
   Turning and returning to some secret place inside;
   Watching in slow motion as you turn to me and say,
   "Take my breath away."

Total Eclipse Of The Heart

Words and Music by Jim Steinman

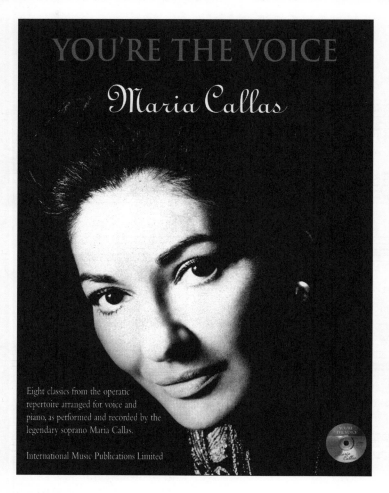

8861A PVC/CD

8860A PVG/CD

Casta Diva from Norma - Vissi D'arte from Tosca
Un Bel Di Vedremo from Madam Butterfly - Addio,
Del Passato from La Traviata - J'ai Perdu Mon
Eurydice from Orphee Et Eurydice - Les Tringles
Des Sistres Tintaient from Carmen - Porgi Amor
from Le Nozze Di Figaro - Ave Maria from Otello

Delilah - Green Green Grass Of Home - Help
Yourself - I'll Never Fall In Love Again - It's Not
Unusual - Mama Told Me Not To Come - Sexbomb
Thunderball - What's New Pussycat - You Can
Leave Your Hat On

YOU'RE THE VOICE

The outstanding new vocal series from IMP

CD contains full backings for each song, professionally arranged to recreate the sounds of the original recording